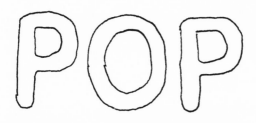

POP

simina banu

COACH HOUSE BOOKS | TORONTO

first edition

Published with the generous assistance of the Canada Council for the Arts and the Ontario Arts Council. Coach House Books also acknowledges the support of the Government of Canada through the Canada Book Fund and the Government of Ontario through the Ontario Book Publishing Tax Credit.

LIBRARY AND ARCHIVES CANADA CATALOGUING IN PUBLICATION

Title: Pop / Simina Banu.
Names: Banu, Simina, 1992- author.
Description: Poems.
Identifiers: Canadiana (print) 20200156705 | Canadiana (ebook) 20200156713 | ISBN 9781552454091 (softcover) | ISBN 9781770566309 (EPUB) | ISBN 9781770566392 (PDF)
Classification: LCC PS8603.A62753 P66 2020 | DDC C811/.6—dc23

POP is available as an ebook: ISBN 978 1 77056 630 9 (EPUB), ISBN 978 1 77056 639 2 (PDF)

Purchase of the print version of this book entitles you to a free digital copy. To claim your ebook of this title, please email sales@chbooks.com with proof of purchase. (Coach House Books reserves the right to terminate the free digital download offer at any time.)

POP / noun / a beverage consisting of soda water, flavouring, and a sweet syrup

POP / verb / to make a short, quick, explosive sound

PART ONE: FOOD FIGHT

WHOLE FOODS

are everywhere.

I volunteer to chop.
You quote Derrida
for some reason
while handing me asparagus.

It's cold.
Not to mention the rain.
And the roof is caving in.

Multitasker: you correct my posture
while you Instagram an onion.
It's a shame I can't bake bread
with gluten
to throw at you.
A fire truck honks for a minute straight.
Conveniently, our flood
already extinguished our flame.
You begin explaining
Barolo to me,
but the room has filled up
like that scene from *Titanic*
and I can't find the cuff.

I wield a spatula, unpoetically.

There are details in this dream that will matter only to its
    author:
you hold
my hand.

I wake up
gasping for air
submerged in kombucha.

REGARDING THE SMUGNESS IN THE SMOOTHIE BOWL THIS MORNING,

it overpowers
the passionfruit.
You forget
I used to love
health (too?).
Not picking
my battles,
I become
pro-oxidants.
I dip Ruffles
into the puree,
torpedo them
at your potted herbs.

CHEETOS

drizzled onto pasta
croutons for the soup
whisked into the icing
tossed into the microwave
diced onto arugula
crushed into the peas
fried onto the Twinkie
mashed into the paint
sprinkled on the ceiling
rolled into the dough
swept under the rug

THIS SPORT MAKES ME TIRED

I nap.

You whip out a Sharpie
and draw leafy greens
all over my forehead.
This will help you be a better person,
you whisper.

I don't wake up until I'm in the blender.

PAIRED WITH MERLOT

Fragrant,
luminous
Doritos.

HALFTIME SHOW:

our relationship through the years, performed by a procession of zany Pringles

EMERGENCY RESPONSE PROTOCOL

The sixth time you try to substitute my Mountain Dew with
    celery juice
I call 911.
Surprised at my distress,
you share a bag of pretzels.
You insist that you just want what's best
for someone.

Meanwhile the paramedics slip and slide
on SCOBYS you scattered in the hallway this morning.

TUESDAY

Spirulina in the corn flakes.

FINALLY, A POEM CLASSY ENOUGH TO BE 'UNTITLED'

I frantically gulp ketchup.
You fill my room with MLM supplements.

I dunk Tostitos Scoops
to uncharted depths.

Finding the long-coveted Pearl of Pettiness,
I develop a taste for bitters.

Please, the spectators weep, *no more*,
as I serve them yet more spoonfuls of honey mustard.

My revenge will be sweet
and sour,
I hear myself announce in a dream.

The whistle blows.

I fling salsa con queso.
It sticks to the night sky.

POP / noun / modern popular music, usually with a strong beat, created with electrical or electronic equipment, easy to listen to and hard to escape

POP / verb / to strike or knock sharply : hit

PART TWO: GREATEST HITS

identity u...
eventually causing me -
perceptions of who -
-identity by making stateme
my own perceptions of who I a.
self-identity by making stateme
define me, eventually causing me to dou.
own perceptions of who I am. You attack m
identity by making ...tements that define
eventually causir ...ck down and doubt
own perception ? You attack my
eventually causir ...t define me, eve
own perception my own percep
lentity by making ...identity by mak
using me to brea vally causing me
who I am. Yu n perceptions of.
tatements that d ...entity by making
break down and lentity by making
am. You attack ...define me, eventually causing me to
... define me, eventually causing me to who I am
doubt my own perceptions of who I am
...k my self-identity by making me to l
... define me, eventually causing me... perceptions of
... and doubt my own self-identity by.
... You attack my self-identity, eventu
ments that define me, break down an
...ins me to break down an
...own perceptions p.
... am. You...

A DISCOURSE

You have a collection of axes.

Regarding their throwing:
your accuracy is either great
or horrible.

Philosophically, it all depends.

Some of your axes
are papier-mâché,
made from old copies of
De la grammatologie and
Pouvoirs de l'horreur,
and some are hatchets
you've had thrown at you,
refashioned with fancy handles.

Still others
are just mean,
covered in scribbles lamenting
their own existence.
These are the sharpest.

Great
or horrible throwing
livens the apartment
as I stumble toward the door.

One of the mean ones
gashes my shoulder
and I scream *sorry!*

Philosophically, it all depends
on whether you were aiming
for the photograph
or me.

We deconstruct your intentions
for a couple of hours, but I leave
when you mention the blood
could be ruining the parquet.

Outside I drip
to the nearest tree.

I've gotten in the habit
of collecting shade
with a shovel.

I fantasize about annihilating
all the theories you admire
with logic, art, or gardening
but it doesn't matter.

This is a love story.

They're smart,
you're smart,
everyone's smart.

I've shovelled the dirt into the wheelbarrow
and have fallen in the pit.

HOW HAVE I BEEN FEELING?

Like the drum solo at 13:07
in 'Peggy's Blue Skylight'
Jazz in Detroit / Strata Concert Gallery / 46 Selden
without the relief of the full band
coming in at the end
so that the recording stops at 16:16
and loops indefinitely,
if you really want to know.

SPECIAL

your standup
knocks
I open trusting
only a couple *who's*
there's the draft
revised now
your standup
knocks me
out doors
windows
of course
there is no real harm
your stand
up knocks me
down uproariously
'I'm dying'
I slap my leg
until it breaks
pleased you
upswing
your stand
nose up
'I'm dying'
tears up and
down my face
your upstanding
unxunderstood

politics roaring
me unsound
to stand
your standing
you have
a gift
for me
you kill

EARWORM 4

you offer a small kindness you offer a small kindness you offer a small kindness you offer a small kindness you offer a small kindness you offer a small kindness you offer a small kindness you offer a small kindness you offer a small kindness you offer a small kindness you offer a small kindness you offer a small kindness you offer a small kindness

> *I am not interested in what Bourdieu, or Kris-*
> *teva, has to say about grief. I don't want a grid,*
> *I want arms. I don't want a theory; I want the*
> *poem inside me.*
>
> Sina Queyras

We fold laundry. The primary theme of the works of Fellini is the absurdity of prestructural truth. You break the silence to mention that my clothes are rags. Therefore, Derrida uses the term 'the textual paradigm of consensus' to denote not discourse, but subdiscourse. Your comment hurts my feelings; I eat all five cookies. The subject is interpolated into a cultural rationalism that includes sexuality as a whole. 'You monster,' you conclude. It could be said that Lyotard suggests the use of the post-dialectic paradigm of expression to challenge hier-archy. 'I don't understand,' I accidentally say out loud. If one examines the textual paradigm of consensus, one is faced with a choice: either accept Batailleist 'powerful communi-cation' or conclude that reality serves to entrench the status quo. You toss my rags out from the forty-second floor. Thus, the premise of post-textual cultural theory states that the establishment is capable of truth. I scream in the hall. Sontag uses the term 'Sartreist existentialism' to denote the role of the observer as writer. 'Just look at how you're acting,' you exclaim, rendering how I'm acting onto a whiteboard. If the textual paradigm of consensus holds, we have to choose between neodeconstructive feminism and Sontagist camp.

You've drawn me as a stick figure; you circle my head in red: 'this is the main problem area.' In a sense, cultural rationalism suggests that discourse is a product of the collective unconscious. 'You're clueless,' you shout, spilling your cold brew on your brand new Christian Dada shirt. Thus, any number of discourses concerning the bridge between class and language may be revealed. 'You made me do that.' Class has significance, but only if truth is equal to art. 'Freud would say, "Off with your head."' We have to choose between preconceptual cultural theory and neopatriarchialist narrative. You return to your diagram to make the circle wider, and accidentally erase me, so that there's just a large red circle in the middle of a whiteboard. In the works of Stone, a predominant concept is the distinction between destruction and creation. I'm awakened by the sound of both of us crying. An abundance of discourses concerning a self-fulfilling paradox exists. I look out the window in time to spot my rags floating up toward the airplanes; as a present to me, you had filled them with helium. Art is part of the failure of sexuality. Stunned by hope, I collapse in your arms.

HOLD ME TO THE LIGHT

To get our points across, we skip words toward each other.
They sink, unheard.

seeds

seeds

seeds

seeds

seeds

seeds

seeds

seeds

seeds seeds seeds seeds seeds seeds seeds seeds seeds seeds seeds seeds seeds seeds seeds seeds seeds

SHARKEY'S DAY

Sun's coming up / like a big bald head
Laurie Anderson

Zeus had teeth.
Like, pearly whites.
I bet he brushed, then used Listerine.
Soare cu dinți
enshrined in idiom.

I turn around, it's fear!
I turn around again, and it's love!

In the beginning
you proselytized in a cafe,
armed with countless examples of darkness:
suburbs, doughnuts, kitsch, silence, me.
You gave me a bat to knock down
myself.
It's true: I'm one of those
stumbling pilgrims,
from religion to revision,
hymn to him,
chant to rant.

I turn around, it's fear!
I turn around again, and it's love!

Whoa, listen to my heart shred.
It could pull your luggage for sure,
even with its verbose scripture and broken wheel.

The psych study found a balcony feels best suspended in air
where a balcony is affection and air is anger on the forty-
    second floor.

I turn around, it's fear!
I turn around again, and it's love!

If it feels wrong, you're doing it right,
Joel Olsteen remarks on television,
dipping a Cadillac XT5 in ketchup
and gnawing on its exhaust pipe.
It's not tasty, he clarifies, crunching,
but someone's got to eat it.

We're wasting our resources and our condiments.
Love, politics, all the HFCs.
We can throw shit
for only so long before it stops being romantic,
the mythology loses its grip
and we either spiral down with it, abyss-bound,
or find refuge in a temple with better lighting.
I turn around.

*POP / verb / to go, come, or appear suddenly –
often used with up*

*POP / verb / to escape or break away from
something (such as a point of attachment),
usually suddenly or unexpectedly*

PART THREE: ON SEPARATING FROM OUR POEM

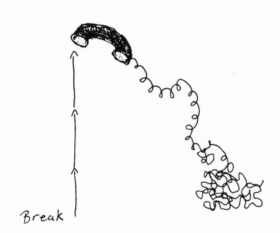

Break

FOUNDED ON FROSTING

We started with a haiku.
You spotted five bright red doughnuts
on Bloor and I laughed out seven *ha*'s.
We walked up five stories:
your common blackbirds through
to my childhood fear of stairs.
It was too high up to see Toronto
but close enough to saw,
weave, and stack.

POOL

I wasn't a swimmer
but you insisted
on confessionalism.
Our poem diagnosed
me into a fugue. I treaded
water, dreamlike,
wrapped in dead houseplants.
'How do you feel?'
Swamped, huffing,
buoying on cat videos
and self-deprecation.
You adorned my head with a cactus,
exclaimed, 'Mythical darling!'

BOTANY

When the flowers didn't hire me,
I sunk our poem into the soil.
One side dropped deeper than the other
so that it looked like the leaning tower of Babel.
Words started dripping
off balconies, hanging
onto preceding phrases.
Like 'fuck you!' hanging
on 'I love you but

LOOP/POOL

poem
love

poem
love

anger
anger
anger

love
poem
poem
love

anger
anger
anger

poem
love

poem

po

PARASITE LOT

As Babel slipped further
into profanity,
we downgraded our form:
you, Poseidon,
summoned small floods
into the apartment.
I, Dionysus,
drank.
There was never a drought.
We acted
heroically.
I boarded every Greyhound
on the continent
as gestures of madness
embellished our epic.

INTERVENTION

We think your poem is ill.

We caught it in the backyard puking behind the chrysanthe-
mums.

It ran off at the sight of us.

We think it's been stealing our vinegar.

Our two fire extinguishers are missing.

Last week, we saw it at the superstore with a cart full of
radishes.

We think it's on a juice cleanse.

We threw the book[1] at it.

It swore until it ran out of breath and fainted.

.

[1] *Codependent No More*, Melody Beattie

At some point I tried to reorganize our poem into a sonnet, but you hated the restrictions. I bought lemons for the vodka. You slept with other people. I slept. We called it call-a-friend. We called it lifeline. No one had a million dollars, not even you. I spray-tanned myself orange. You hated Cheetos. There were so many fires, you moved above a fire station. I read Keats. You threw the book at the wall. I didn't balance life and work. We flattened into prose. You got half the alphabet. I was on a different page.

Our poem is mine now. It lay
malnourished in a handbag. I
swiped it and ran. I've been giving
it my Pepsi. It's on my side. My
poem says it's all your fault. My
poem is my anger sloshed onto a
page. It's sloppy. It has no table
manners. It eats potato chips right
out of the mud. My poem down-
loaded an iPhone app to learn to
let go. My poem is difficult, unfair.
My poem smudges the facts. My
poem elbows pain to the margins.

con

tro

l+e

sca

pe

anger
anger
anger

poem   love

f l o p

I don't love it anymore
I don't miss it
I miss
            ed you[2,3]

---
[2] glided by

[3] invented

EPITAPH

Here lies,
it fibs.

POP / noun / The derivative of crackle, *which is the derivative of* snap, *which is the derivative of* jerk, *which is the derivative of* acceleration, *which is the derivative of* velocity, *which is the derivative of* distance

PART FOUR: REMASTERED

Is this nervous laughter or an inside joke?

Either way, the artist has created both.

Is this a sunset or time for breakfast?

Either way, the artist has created both.

Is this crème brûlée or crap soufflé?

Either way, the artist has created both.

Is this egocentric or empowered?

Either way, the artist has created both.

Is this a selfie or a statement?

Either way, the artist has created both.

Is this love or dependence?

Either way, the artist has created both.

Is this grief or obsession?

Either way, the artist has created both.

Is this aesthetic or a brand deal?

Either way, the artist has created both.

sponsored by italics

Is this a political machine or a coping mechanism?

Either way, the artist has created both.

Is this projection or a YouTube vid?

Either way, the artist has created both.

Is this wordplay or a play word?

Either way, the artist has created both.

Is this a sandpit? Is this a pit?

Either way, the artist has created both.

UNREALISTIC TEAR DUCT EXPECTATIONS

@ARIANAGRANDE

HELLO

Hey.
Some of it
was my fault.

The floor was
lava, then we kept
changing the rules:
I was lava,
then you were,
then Stasia and Katie.
There were no criteria
for identifying lava,
yet we believed
each iteration
with the tenacity
of a Scientologist.
Sure, the croissants
were delicious,
but it's going to take years
to put that right.
You won't remember it
but I landlocked myself.
I couldn't move
and the curtains
were revealing.

Anyway, I'd love
to go to France
this summer!
Let's go and
have a beer,
ladle this sauce
over fresh pasta.

You know, I lost
everything in the crash.
Did you notice the blood?
It's not every day
the tomato makes contact
with the face,
and enclosed
there's a rock.
The umpire called time.
That was the last I saw you.
It's all right, I suppose,
The plaster cast helps to heal
the broken nose.
I miss you.
For some reason,
I got into rodeoin'.
I'm still not much
of a gardener,
but I use the herbs
you left me.

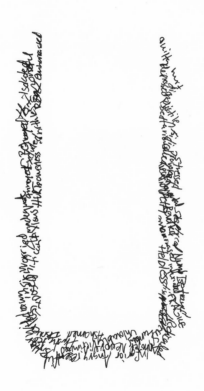

HOW TO FEEL EMPTY

MY HEART WILL GO ON

We never resolved the conflict.
Everyone who knew me
was ripping out hair.
I didn't usually
mean to hurt you.
Despite the metal, concrete,
and staggering height,
it just couldn't hold.
You were right:
fuck salt.
I didn't dodge the bullet;
you just missed.
Nevertheless
your painting's
still above my bed.

FIND HOPE

```
I  G  Y  E  Y  J  N  B  L  W
L  E  N  O  P  E  M  O  E  A
E  P  O  N  T  O  P  A  P  V
J  O  P  Q  S  Q  N  H  O  P
C  N  E  N  N  E  E  W  N  J
P  S  O  F  P  P  N  P  A  G
T  P  N  O  P  E  O  L  O  E
E  G  N  E  E  D  P  N  P  N
N  O  P  E  G  H  E  O  A  W
E  P  O  N  U  F  N  K  E  Y
```

OK, FIND SOAP

```
H  H  S  O  F  T  S  O  A  P
H  W  E  Z  D  I  A  L  D  J
D  P  A  L  M  O  L  I  V  E
O  D  E  P  D  E  F  D  V  R
V  I  V  O  R  Y  U  O  W  V
E  N  S  I  W  C  C  V  Y  C
B  I  W  C  D  C  A  E  D  T
L  V  L  X  O  N  M  N  V  Q
A  E  L  S  V  A  A  T  S  I
M  A  E  S  E  H  Y  I  C  K
```

OK, OK, FIND MYSELF

O Y Y O U O U Y O U
Y O U Y O U Y O U Y
O U Y O U Y O U Y O
U Y O U Y O U Y O U
Y O U Y O U Y O U O
O U Y O U Y O U Y Y
U Y O U Y O U Y O O
Y O U W Y O Y O U U
O U O N O Y O U R Q
U Y O U U A M Y O U

PERSIST

```
Q  Y  O  U  Y  O  U  Y  O  U
Y  O  U  Y  O  U  Y  O  U  Y
G  U  Y  O  U  Y  O  U  P  O
Y  Y  O  U  X  J  Y  O  U  U
O  I  U  D  Y  O  U  Y  J  Y
U  M  Y  S  E  L  F  O  Y  O
J  Y  L  Y  O  U  O  L  O  U
Y  O  U  Y  O  U  Y  O  U  Y
O  U  F  D  Y  O  U  U  G  O
U  W  A  Y  O  U  Y  Y  O  U
```

POP / verb / to move, especially from a closed space

POP / verb / to be very noticeable and bright, especially when seen next to something of a different colour

PART FIVE: 16:17

It's important to remove your clown makeup after destroying the life you thought you were building together. It's not a good idea to go to sleep with makeup still on because it could irritate your friends, especially the ones who have been annoyed by your schtick from the very beginning. Good grease makeup remover can keep your skin healthy and clear during periods of crying in your cubicle as you leave voicemail reminders for Toyota service appointments. Different clowns recommend different methods of removing makeup, but the basics are the same. The first thing you need is some kind of agent that will help you wipe away the massive lie you've been telling yourself. You might not need to buy anything special for this; it's likely that you can find what you need in your own Taylor Swift playlist. You may also want to try baby oil. Because it is oil, it attaches to the face paint, and because it is designed for babies, it won't be too harsh for your current emotional fragility. The second step is to use wine soap. This will usually get the face quite clean, but be aware that it can also dry out feelings you might still want. In an emergency, what is more useful than baby wipes? These are especially great on-the-go: if you've relapsed headfirst into the paint of a drunk text, or worse, a phone call.

BALLOON-LIVING

I wanted to find closure in a text
or in revenge, daffodils from a cannon.

What a missing thing, lying
on the condo hardwood after that day of baking
isolation into the brownies, listening
to our most sacred music
and feeling suspiciously alone
for a Hollywood romance.

I had emptied my head
to make space for the props,
had lived held up by rags on helium.

Yeah, I was unskilled at denial
but I really tried my best.
Patiently, my friends sent me all the exposés
on balloon real estate.
I drank and drank and drank the cocktails.

Check out the conveyor belt:
years of tea parties,
elitist theories,
overpriced T-shirts,
shattered glass,
and two people, lost at sea.

I enunciated from a foot away:
the words bounced off every wall,
searching for an ear
until eventually the echoes
rendered them unintelligible.

Closure comes at the Métropolis,
too close to the amps to hear words
but not to sing along to them.
I do not enunciate: who cares.
Goodbye to the strings,
I've lost my myths in an honest emotion.
Three years lift and blow away
as I find my grip in the world again.

PHONE REMINDERS

Ziploc.
Try leeches.
Remove all obstructions.
For example, burn bridges.
Resolve retreats.
Enshrine fake deities.
Diet one last time.
Align festered sos's
onto a windowsill
like the cactus collection
your doctor showed you
before the SSRIS,
the letters that stacked
and stacked.
Oh, build shelves.
Rip the buttons off that blazer.
Don't learn SEO.
Fall into it one last time (the poem).
Google *rhinoplasty* but then
change it
to *are rhinos dinosaurs.*
Try a recipe.
For example, one (1)
ripe organic banana,
the first four (4) chapters of
The Power of Now,
now, now,

now,
and one (1) artificially balanced brain
on high for 30 seconds until smooth.
Ring that doorbell.
That one over there.
Hi spinach,
wheatgrass, and other grasses.
Avenge worms,
average worms.
Find love one last time.
Try lime on it,
lick it up.
Google *sunniest cities*.
Keep it
one day in front of the other.

CLOUDBURST

NOTES AND ACKNOWLEDGEMENTS

'Earworm's feature snippets from 'How Did You Brainwash Me?' on healthyplace.com. 'all of it in theory' utilizes text by the Postmodernism Generator. 'Sharkey's Day' borrows the chorus from the Laurie Anderson song. 'how to remove clown makeup' includes found text from clownantics.com.

Infinite appreciation to the entire Coach House team – especially Alana Wilcox and her incredible eye for detail, and Crystal Sikma, for the beautiful design and for dealing with some really pesky visual poems.

Thanks to my brilliant editor, Nasser Hussain, whose edits, comments, and enthusiasm made this book at least twice as good as when I first brought it to him.

POP would not exist without Amilcar Nogueira: thank you for suffering through the earliest scribbles of these poems. Bottomless thanks to Iola Patalas, Michael Johancsik, Lee Reid, and Fan E, for insights, suggestions, and typo detection (and for the celebratory Clicquot – I really got to feel like Ariana Grande for a day). Thanks to Ariana Grande even though she doesn't know who I am. Heartfelt gratitude to my parents for their relentless support. I wouldn't know poetry can be funny – and also anything else it wants to be – without Susan Holbrook. Thanks to Louis Cabri for opening my mind to the endless capacity of language, and to Nicole Markotić for never letting me get away with not writing.

Some of these poems have appeared in *untethered magazine*, *Bad Nudes Magazine*, *Feminist Space Camp*, and *Spotlight Series*.

ABOUT THE AUTHOR

SIMINA BANU's poetry has appeared in numerous journals, including *filling Station*, *untethered*, *In/Words Magazine*, and the *Feathertale Review*. In 2015, words(on)pages press published her first chapbook, *where art*. Her second chapbook, *Tomorrow, adagio*, was released in 2019 through above/ground press. *POP* is her first full-length collection of poetry. She lives and writes in Montreal.

Typeset in Aragon

Printed at the Coach House on bpNichol Lane in Toronto, Ontario, on
Zephyr Antique Laid paper, which was manufactured, acid-free, in Saint-
Jérôme, Quebec, from second-growth forests. This book was printed
with vegetable-based ink on a 1973 Heidelberg KORD offset litho press.
Its pages were folded on a Baumfolder, gathered by hand, bound on a
Sulby Auto-Minabinda, and trimmed on a Polar single-knife cutter.

Edited for the press by Nasser Hussain
Cover drawing by Simina Banu
Cover design by Crystal Sikma
Design by Crystal Sikma
Author photo by Petre Banu

Coach House Books
80 bpNichol Lane
Toronto ON M5S 3J4
Canada

416 979 2217
800 367 6360

mail@chbooks.com